It's Always

Spritz
O'Clock

Somewhere

It's Always

Spritz

O'Clock

CLASSIC
COCKTAIL
RECIPES FROM
WHERE YOU'D
RATHER BE

Somewhere

Harper *by* Design

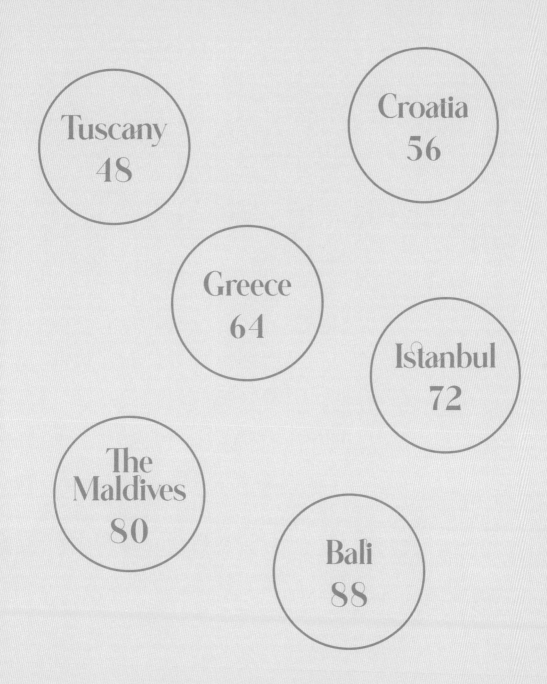

Tuscany
48

Croatia
56

Greece
64

Istanbul
72

The
Maldives
80

Bali
88

Ready, Steady ... Spritz!

No matter whether you're at an airport bar waiting to jet off on a Bali beach break or at home on your couch dreaming of cruising the Mediterranean Sea aboard a yacht, one sure-fire way to slip into holiday mode is to raise a spritz to your lips.

The drink of choice at boozy brunches, long lunches, summer picnics, pool parties and beyond, a spritz signifies the start of something good. From a classy Champagne Cocktail at a ritzy hotel bar on the French Riviera to a bittersweet Negroni Sbagliato at a rustic Tuscan trattoria, sipping a sneaky spritz has universal appeal wherever you are in the world.

A zero-drama tipple that's easy to whip up (and even easier to drink), spritz proves that you only need a few ingredients to make a big impact. Let this companion guide take you on a journey to some of the world's dreamiest locations – places made even more perfect when paired with a spritz.

Whether you're a new convert or a die-hard spritz fan from way back, take inspiration from these recipes and inject some fizzy magic into your life.

Go on, get your spritz on.

Palm

Springs

Palm Springs ~ California ~ 12:24pm

Palm Springs   ~   California   ~   2:07pm

Palm Springs ~ California ~ 3:51pm

The blue-sky city that hangs its hat on mid-century modernism also embraces happy-hour drinks with gusto. Whether it's mid-morning, lunchtime, afternoon or evening, there's no better way to counter the dry desert heat than with an ice-cold Aperol Spritz (or two).

Aperol Spritz

50ml Aperol
100ml prosecco
25ml soda water
ice
slice of orange,
  to garnish

Fill a wine glass with ice. Pour the Aperol and prosecco into the glass, then top up with soda water. Stir gently and garnish with an orange slice.

~
SERVED WITH
ICE IN A WINE
GLASS

~

SAY *CHEERS*
TO TOAST!

Cuba

Havana   ~   Cuba   ~   2:56pm

Viñales   ~   Cuba   ~   3:29pm

After a long day spent wandering around Old Havana gawking at the city's vintage cars and eclectic architecture (Art Deco! Cuban Baroque! Neoclassical!), beat the heat with this tangy tipple best savoured with a sea breeze. Just like the nation of Cuba, this refreshing spritz will salsa its way straight into your heart.

Bicicletta

50ml Campari
100ml dry white
  wine
25ml soda water
ice
slice of orange,
  to garnish

Fill a wine glass with ice. Pour the Campari and wine into the glass, then top up with soda water. Stir gently, then garnish with an orange slice.

~

SERVED WITH
ICE IN A WINE
GLASS

~

SAY *SALUD*
TO TOAST!

Buenos

Aires

Casa Rosada   ~   Buenos Aires   ~   12:11pm

Caminito　　　~　　　Buenos Aires　　　~　　　1:38pm

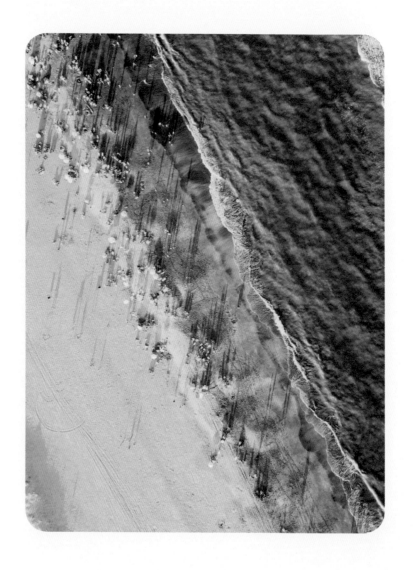

Costa Esmeralda ~ Buenos Aires ~ 2:47pm

Life's a peach when you kick off proceedings with this sweet, effervescent breakfast-friendly spritz named after a Renaissance-era painter. Pair it with Argentina's favourite breakfast: a buttery, flaky, warm pastry fresh from the local bakery. *Delicioso!*

Bellini

25ml peach
  puree
140ml prosecco
slice of peach,
  to garnish

To make the
peach puree:
2 peaches
25ml sugar
  syrup

Peel the peaches then blend them with the sugar syrup until smooth. Pour the puree into a champagne flute, followed by the prosecco. Stir gently and garnish with a slice of fresh peach.

~

SERVED IN A
CHAMPAGNE
FLUTE

~

SAY *SALUD*
TO TOAST!

Barcelona

Barceloneta Beach ~ Barcelona ~ 11:39am

Tibidabo   ~   Barcelona   ~   4:58pm

Llevant Beach   ~   Barcelona   ~   5:45pm

An enduring brunch favourite that legitimises morning drinking, the two-ingredient Mimosa is dead easy to make. Whether you're toasting a milestone with mates or enjoying solo with a Spanish omelette, starting the day with the classic combo of champagne and OJ is a power move you'll never regret.

Mimosa

75ml sparkling wine or champagne
75ml freshly squeezed orange juice

Fill a champagne flute halfway with sparkling wine (or champagne if you're feeling fancy), then fill the rest of the flute with orange juice.

~

SERVED IN A CHAMPAGNE FLUTE

~

SAY *SALUD* TO TOAST!

French
Riviera

Villefranche-sur-Mer   -   French Riviera   -   1:36pm

Synonymous with superyachts, sunshine and seriously wealthy people, the Côte d'Azur is catnip for cashed-up celebrities. Luckily, you don't need to be famous to enjoy a classic Champagne Cocktail. Just make this refreshing tipple anytime you need an afternoon pick-me-up with a touch of class.

Champagne Cocktail

1 sugar cube
$\frac{1}{4}$ tsp Angostura bitters
10ml cognac
90ml champagne or sparkling wine
orange peel, to garnish

Place the sugar cube in the champagne flute, then soak the sugar cube with bitters. Add the cognac, then pour in the champagne. Garnish with orange peel.

~

SERVED IN A CHAMPAGNE FLUTE

~

SAY SANTÉ TO TOAST!

Tuscany

Florence ～ Tuscany ～ 4:09pm

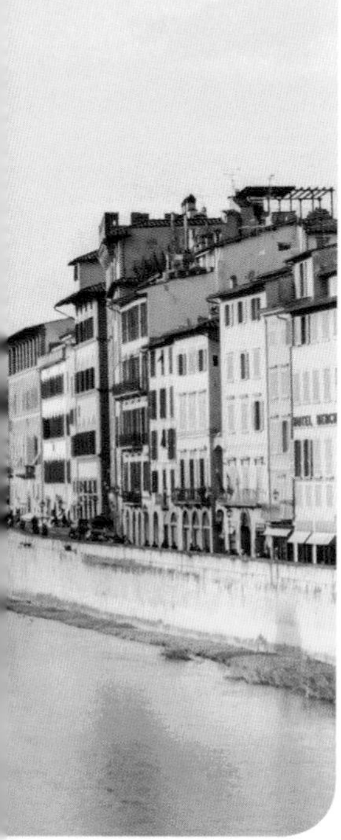

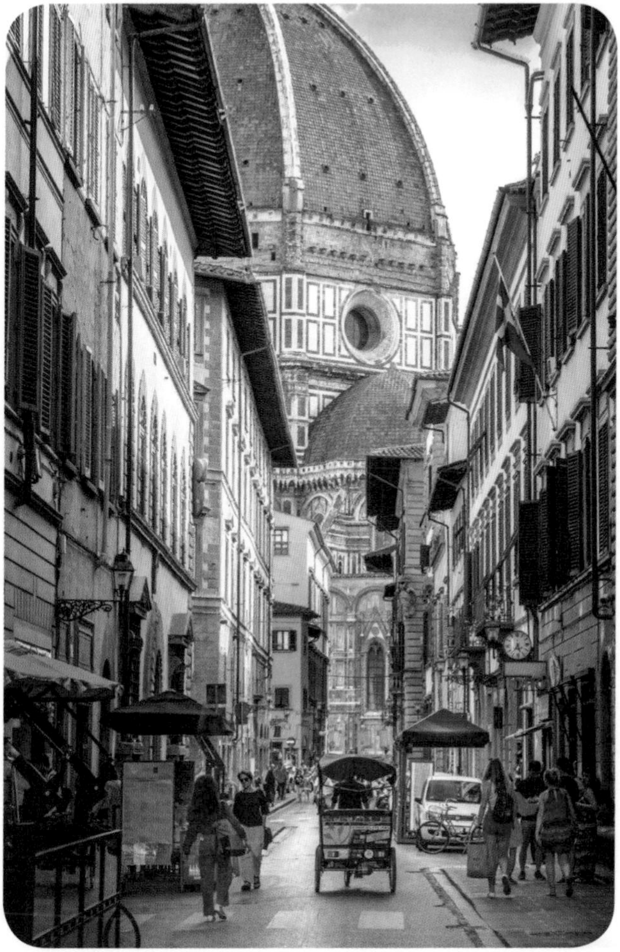

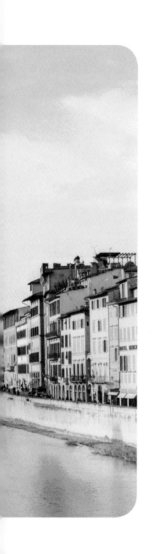

Siena   ~   Tuscany   ~   6:58pm

Tuscan villa ownership isn't required to enjoy the great Italian tradition of the aperitivo hour. After a long day at work, crank some Dean Martin tunes and kick back with this light and fizzy alternative to a full-blown Negroni. It's the perfect pre-dinner libation to take the edge off your day.

Negroni Sbagliato

30ml Campari
30ml sweet
  vermouth
30ml prosecco
ice
slice of dried
  orange, to
  garnish

Fill a glass with ice. Add the Campari, sweet vermouth and prosecco, then give the mixture a gentle stir. Garnish with a slice of dried orange.

~

SERVED IN A
SHORT GLASS
TUMBLER WITH ICE

~

SAY *CIN CIN*
TO TOAST!

Croatia

Dubrovnik ~ Croatia ~ 1:47pm

Rovinj ~ Croatia ~ 3:58pm

Hvar   ~   Croatia   ~   4:11pm

Impress your friends with some spritz trivia by whipping up this sweet bevvy named after Félix Kir, a priest and hero of the French Resistance during World War II. Whether you're entertaining at home or toasting a dazzling Dubrovnik sunset, this juicy, berry-rich tipple will hit the spot.

Kir Royale

1 tbsp crème
  de cassis
150ml champagne
  or sparkling wine
1 fresh blackberry,
  to garnish

Pour the crème de cassis into the bottom of the glass, then top up with champagne or sparkling wine. Garnish with a blackberry.

~
SERVED IN A
CHAMPAGNE
FLUTE

~
SAY ŽIVJELI
TO TOAST!

Greece

Santorini ~ Greece ~ 12:53pm

Milos ~ Greece ~ 1:22pm

Kefalonia ~ Greece ~ 2:04pm

Transport yourself to the balmy Mediterranean with this heady, bittersweet summer spritz. Reminiscent of holidays by the sea and long lunches under a lemon-tree canopy, this fragrant flavour bomb is sunshine in a glass.

Limoncello Spritz

50ml limoncello
60ml prosecco
30ml soda water
ice
slice of lemon,
  to garnish

Fill a wine glass with ice. Pour in the limoncello, then add the prosecco. Top up with soda water and gently stir. Garnish with a slice of lemon.

~

SERVED WITH
ICE IN A WINE
GLASS

~

SAY *YIA MAS*
TO TOAST!

Istanbul

Ortaköy ～ Istanbul ～ 5:40pm

Karaköy   ~   Istanbul   ~   6:16pm

Sultanahmet ~ Istanbul ~ 8:10pm

Earthy, aromatic and bittersweet, Cynar is as unique, complex and enthralling as the city of Istanbul itself, and something of an under-the-radar choice to add to your liqueur repertoire. Mix it with prosecco and soda water and you've got yourself a new go-to drink to down before dinner.

Cynar Spritz

50ml Cynar
50ml prosecco
50ml soda
  water
ice
slice of orange,
  to garnish

Pour the Cynar, prosecco and soda water into a wine glass with ice. Mix gently and garnish with a slice of orange.

~
SERVED WITH
ICE IN A WINE
GLASS

~

SAY ŞEREFE
TO TOAST!

The

Maldives

Himandhoo　　　-　　　The Maldives　　　-　　　2:19pm

You know what goes perfectly with watching a sublime sunset from an overwater bungalow? A white wine spritzer.* Luckily, water-bound luxury accommodation isn't a prerequisite for enjoying this popular all-rounder. Bust it out at barbecues, picnics and lazy afternoons on the deck – the white wine spritzer knows no bounds.

White Wine Spritzer

125ml dry
 riesling or
 sauvignon blanc
30ml soda water
ice
slice of lime, to
 garnish

Add ice to a wine glass. Pour the chilled wine into the glass, top up with soda water and garnish with a slice of lime.

~
SERVED WITH
ICE IN A WINE GLASS

~

SAY *CHEERS*
TO TOAST!

* A traditional Germanic spin on the spritz, a spritzer is made with white wine rather than bubbly.

Bali

Ubud   ~   Bali   ~   11:08am

Nusa Penida　　～　　Bali　　～　　2:49pm

After a day of organic green juices, vegan smoothie bowls and hot-yoga classes, complete your Bali retreat with a refreshing Campari Spritz by your villa's plunge pool.
After all, you can't achieve peak wellness without a little thing called balance.

Campari Spritz

60ml Campari
90ml prosecco
20ml soda water
ice
slice of orange,
 to garnish

Add ice to a wine glass. Pour in the Campari, prosecco and soda water. Gently stir then garnish with a slice of orange.

~

SERVED WITH ICE IN A WINE GLASS

~

SAY *BERSULANG* TO TOAST!

Harper *by* Design
An imprint of HarperCollins*Publishers*

HarperCollins*Publishers*
Australia • Brazil • Canada • France • Germany • Holland • India
Italy • Japan • Mexico • New Zealand • Poland • Spain • Sweden
Switzerland • United Kingdom • United States of America

HarperCollins acknowledges the Traditional Custodians of the land upon which we live and work,
and pays respect to Elders past and present.

First published in Australia in 2022
by HarperCollins*Publishers* Australia Pty Limited
Gadigal Country
Level 13, 201 Elizabeth Street, Sydney NSW 2000
ABN 36 009 913 517
harpercollins.com.au

A catalogue record for this book is available from the National Library of Australia.

ISBN 978 1 4607 6256 1

Publisher: Mark Campbell
Publishing Director: Brigitta Doyle
Editor: Scott Forbes
Copywriter: Jo Stewart
Designer: Mietta Yans, HarperCollins Design Studio
Front cover image by Wildroze/iStock
Back cover images by Fermin Rodriguez Penelas/Unsplash; Ryan Spencer/Unsplash; Marco Da Silva/Unsplash
Internal photographs courtesy of Unsplash, except as noted: page 8 Thinkreaction/iStock;
10 2M media/Shutterstock; 12 Jon Bilous/Shutterstock; 12 Goodluz/Shutterstock; 13 Wildroze/iStock;
14 Lindsay Bernacchi/iStock; 27 Luoman/iStock; 29 Jess Kraft/Shutterstock; 44 Milena Pigdanowicz-Fidera/iStock;
44 Nikitje/iStock; 45 StockByM/iStock; 54 Joci03/iStock; 70 Miniloc/iStock
Colour reproduction by Splitting Image Colour Studio, Clayton VIC
Printed and bound in China by RR Donnelley

8 7 6 5 4 3 2 1   22 23 24 25